BIN LADEN Usama
A-268/5-1998

I0417736

PRESENT FAMILY NAME: BIN LADEN

FORENAME: Usama   SEX: M

DATE AND PLACE OF BIRTH: 1957 - Jeddah, Saudi Arabia

FATHER'S FORENAMES: Abdulrahamn 'Awadh

IDENTITY CONFIRMED - NATIONALITY: SAUDI ARABIAN (CONFIRMED)

LANGUAGE SPOKEN: Arabic.

ACCOMPLICES:

AL-'ALWAN Faraj Mikhaïl Abdul-Fadeel Jibril, born in 1969, subject of red notice File No. 1998/20220, Control No. A-270/5-1998;

AL-WARFALI Faez Abu Zeid Muftah, born in 1968, subject of red notice File No. 1998/20223, Control No. A-271/5-1998;

AL-CHALABI Faraj, born in 1966, subject of red notice File No. 1998/20230, Control No. A-269/5-1998.

SUMMARY OF FACTS OF THE CASE: LIBYA: On 10th March 1994, BIN LADEN, AL-CHALABI, AL-'ALWAN and AL-WARFALI killed two German nationals near Surt.

REASON FOR NOTICE: Wanted on arrest warrant No. 1.27.288/1998, issued on 16th March 1998 by the judicial authorities in Tripoli, Libya, for murder and illegal possession of firearms.

EXTRADITION WILL BE REQUESTED FROM ANY COUNTRY EXCEPT ISRAEL.

If found in a country from which extradition will be requested, please detain; if found elsewhere, please keep a watch on his movements and activities. In either case, immediately inform INTERPOL TRIPOLI (Reference 6.27.8497.352 of 15th April 1998) and the ICPO-Interpol General Secretariat.

Refer to FBI

19

File No. 1998/20232   Control No. A-268/5-1998

BIN LADEN Usama
A-268/5-1998

PRESENT FAMILY NAME: BIN LADEN

FORENAME: Usama   SEX: M

DATE AND PLACE OF BIRTH: 1957 - Jeddah, Saudi Arabia

FATHER'S FORENAMES: Abdulrahamn 'Awadh

IDENTITY CONFIRMED - NATIONALITY: SAUDI ARABIAN (CONFIRMED)

LANGUAGE SPOKEN: Arabic.

ACCOMPLICES:

AL-'ALWAN Faraj Mikhaïl Abdul-Fadeel Jibril, born in 1969, subject of red notice File No. 1998/20220, Control No. A-270/5-1998;

AL-WARFALI Faez Abu Zeid Muftah, born in 1968, subject of red notice File No. 1998/20223, Control No. A-271/5-1998;

AL-CHALABI Faraj, born in 1966, subject of red notice File No. 1998/20230, Control No. A-269/5-1998.

SUMMARY OF FACTS OF THE CASE: LIBYA: On 10th March 1994, BIN LADEN, AL-CHALABI, AL-'ALWAN and AL-WARFALI killed two German nationals near Surt.

REASON FOR NOTICE: Wanted on arrest warrant No. 1.27.288/1998, issued on 16th March 1998 by the judicial authorities in Tripoli, Libya, for murder and illegal possession of firearms.

EXTRADITION WILL BE REQUESTED FROM ANY COUNTRY EXCEPT ISRAEL.

If found in a country from which extradition will be requested, please detain; if found elsewhere, please keep a watch on his movements and activities. In either case, immediately inform INTERPOL TRIPOLI (Reference 6.27.8497.352 of 15th April 1998) and the ICPO-Interpol General Secretariat.

Refer to P.G.I

File No. 1998/20232   Control No. A-268/5-1998

BIN LADEN Usama
A-268/5-1998

PRESENT FAMILY NAME: BIN LADEN

FORENAME: Usama   SEX: M

DATE AND PLACE OF BIRTH: 1957 - Jeddah, Saudi Arabia

FATHER'S FORENAMES: Abdulrahamn 'Awadh

<u>IDENTITY CONFIRMED - NATIONALITY: SAUDI ARABIAN (CONFIRMED)</u>

<u>LANGUAGE SPOKEN</u>: Arabic.

<u>ACCOMPLICES</u>:

AL-'ALWAN Faraj Mikhaïl Abdul-Fadeel Jibril, born in 1969, subject of red notice File No. 1998/20220, Control No. A-270/5-1998;

AL-WARFALI Faez Abu Zeid Muftah, born in 1968, subject of red notice File No. 1998/20223, Control No. A-271/5-1998;

AL-CHALABI Faraj, born in 1966, subject of red notice File No. 1998/20230, Control No. A-269/5-1998.

<u>SUMMARY OF FACTS OF THE CASE</u>: LIBYA: On 10th March 1994, BIN LADEN, AL-CHALABI, AL-'ALWAN and AL-WARFALI killed two German nationals near Surt.

<u>REASON FOR NOTICE</u>: Wanted on arrest warrant No. 1.27.288/1998, issued on 16th March 1998 by the judicial authorities in Tripoli, Libya, for murder and illegal possession of firearms.

EXTRADITION WILL BE REQUESTED FROM ANY COUNTRY EXCEPT ISRAEL.

If found in a country from which extradition will be requested, please detain; if found elsewhere, please keep a watch on his movements and activities. In either case, immediately inform INTERPOL TRIPOLI (Reference 6.27.8497.352 of 15th April 1998) and the ICPO-Interpol General Secretariat.

Refer to FBI

File No. 1998/20232   **Control No. A-268/5-1998**

PRIORITY: Normal

DATE: 6 March 2000

FROM: Interpol Washington

OUR REF: ▓▓▓▓▓▓ b2, b7C INTERPOL - USNCB

SUBJECT: BIN LADEN, f/n Usama; born in 1957

RedHead   PERSON WANTED FOR PROSECUTION

1.   IDENTITY PARTICULARS

WARNING: THIS PERSON MAY BE:
    Armed
    Dangerous

1.1   PRESENT FAMILY NAME:
      Bin Laden

1.2   FAMILY NAME AT BIRTH / PREVIOUS FAMILY NAMES:
      Bin Laden

1.3   FORENAMES:
      Usama,

1.4   SEX:
      M

1.5   DATE AND PLACE OF BIRTH:
      Date Unknown, 1957
      Jeddah,
      Saudi Arabia

1.6   FATHER'S FAMILY NAME AND FORENAMES:
      Bin Laden,   Abdul Rahamn Awadh

1.7   MOTHER'S MAIDEN NAME AND FORENAMES:
      not known

Refer to FBI

1.8   RESULT OF IDENTITY CHECK:
        IDENTITY CONFIRMED

1.9   NATIONALITY(IES):
        Saudi Arabia ...   (CONFIRMED)

1.10   IDENTITY DOCUMENTS:
        Passport Number: not known
        Other Identification Information:
        none known

1.11   ALSO KNOWN AS:
        Usamah Bin Muhammad Bin Laden; Shaykh Usamah Bin Ladin; Abu Abdullah; Mujahid
Shaykh; Hajj; al Qaqa; "the Director.

1.12   DESCRIPTION:
        Height: 195.6 cm
        Weight: 67.5 kg
        Hair Color: Black
        Eye Color: Brown
        Complexion: Medium

1.13   DISTINQUISHING MARKS AND CHARACTERISTICS:
        Usually wears full beard and mustache, may walk with a cane.

1.14   OCCUPATION:
        Religious Cleric; Arms Dealer

1.15   LANGUAGES SPOKEN:
        Arabic

1.16   REGIONS/COUNTRIES LIKELY TO BE VISITED:
        Middle East; Southwest Asia

1.17   ADDITIONAL INFORMATION:
        Also the subject of Red Notice Control Number A-268/5-1998, File Number 1998/20232
issued at the request of IP Libya for killing two German nationals in 1994.

2.   JUDICIAL INFORMATION

2.1   SUMMARY OF FACTS OF THE CASE:
        BIN LADEN is wanted for his role in the bombing of United States Embassies in Kenya
and Tanzania on 7th August 1998. BIN LADEN was a leader of "al Qaeda," a group that
conspired to commit violent acts against the United States. Specifically, on 23 August 1996, BIN
LADEN signed and issued a declaration of jihad against Americans in the Arabian peninsula,

authorizing his followers to commit violent acts against the U.S. In February, 1998 BIN LADEN
endorsed a fatwah authorizing the killing of American civilians anywhere in the world where
they can be found. The substance of these were repeated by Bin Laden during a press conference
in May, 1998. During July and August, 1998 members of "al Qaeda" made preparations to
detonate explosives near the U.S. embassies in Kenya and Tanzania. The embassies were
actually bombed on 7 August 1998. More than 216 lives were lost in the Kenya explosion and
more than 10 lives were lost in the explosion in Tanzania.

2.2   ACCOMPLICES:
Muhammad Atef; Wadih El Hage; Mohamed Sadeek Odeh; Mohamed Rashed Daoud
Al-Owhali; Mustafa Mohamed Fadhil; Khalfan Khamis Mohamed; Ahmed Khalfan Ghailani;
Sheikh Ahmed Salim Swedan;Msalam, f/n Fahid, Mohammed Ally

2.3   CHARGE:
Murder; Murder Conspiracy; Attack on a United States Facility

2.4   LAW COVERING THE OFFENCE:
Title 18 United States Code Sections 2332(b), 844(f) and 930(a)

2.5   MAXIMUM PENALTY POSSIBLE:
Life in prison

2.6   TIME-LIMIT FOR ENFORCEMENT: None

2.7   ARREST WARRANT:
No. S(2) 98 CR. 1023 issued on 16 December 1998
by the judicial authorities in United States District Court, Southern District of New York;
New York, New York (USA)
Name of signatory: Theodore Katz, United States Magistrate Judge

2.8   RECORD OF CONVICTION / SENTENCE AVAILABLE AT THE GENERAL
SECRETARIAT IN THE LANGUAGE USED BY THE REQUESTING COUNTRY: NO

3 - ACTION TO BE TAKEN IF FUGITIVE IS FOUND
PROVISIONAL ARREST

It is understood that:
- the NCB of the country where the wanted person is found should immediately inform the
requesting NCB (quoting reference and date) and the General Secretariat;
- if that country considers red notices to be valid requests for provisional arrest, the fugitive
should be provisionally arrested.

EXTRADITION

Please tick the wording required (before asking for publication of a red notice, the requesting

PRIORITY: Normal (Important)

DATE: 7 Dec 1998

FROM: Interpol Washington

TO: Interpol ███████ b7   **INTERPOL - USNCB**

OUR REF: ███████████ b2, b7

CC: Investigating Agency: FBI
             Prosecuting Agency: U.S. ATTORNEY'S OFFICE
             Office of International Affairs, US Department of Justice

YOUR REF: New Inquiry

REGARDING: Fugitive Broadcast - BIN LADEN, F/N USAMA

ASF: No Exclusions

THIS IS A RETRANSMISSION OF OUR PREVIOUS DIFFUSION DATED 4 DECEMBER 1998 WHICH AMENDS THE OCCUPATION OF THE SUBJECT.

On behalf of the FBI please locate the following fugitive and immediately notify Interpol Washington and IPSG. Upon notification, U.S. authorities will, if possible, formally request provisional arrest with a view toward extradition in accordance with any applicable extradition treaty.

Present Family Name: BIN LADEN

Family Name at Birth: BIN LADEN

First Name: USAMA

Date of Birth: 1957

Approximate Age: 41

Place of Birth: JEDDAH, SAUDI ARABIA

Nationality(ies): SAUDI ARABIAN

Alias(es):
        USAMA BIN LADEN, AKA
        USAMAH BIN-MUHAMMAD BIN-LADIN
        SHAYKH USAMA BIN-LADIN
        ABU ABDULLAH
        MUJAHID SHAYKH
        HAJJ

Name of Father: BIN LADEN, ABDUL RAHAMN AWADH

Name of Mother: NOT AVAILABLE

Skin Tone: Olive

Height: 195.58 CM / 6 FT 5 IN

Weight: 61.376 KG / 137 POUNDS

Eye Color: Brown

Hair Color: Brown

Physical Descriptors: FULL BEARD, MUSTACHE, WALKS WITH CANE

Language(s) Spoken: ARABIC

Occupation: FORMERLY CONSTRUCTION EXECUTIVE AND CURRENTLY LEADER OF A
          TERRORIST ORGANIZATION KNOWN AS AL-QAEDA.

Areas likely to be visited: MIDDLE EAST, WESTERN EUROPE

Passport: NOT AVAILABLE

Misc. ID: NOT AVAILABLE

Fingerprints: Not Available

Photograph: Attached

Caution/Warning:
          ARMED AND DANGEROUS

Arrest Warrant Number: S(2)98CR.1023

Arrest Date: 04 NOV 1998

By (Judge): JAMES M. PARKISON, U.S. DISTRICT COURT SOUTHERN DISTRICT
OF NEW YORK

City and State: NEW YORK, NEW YORK

Name of Offense(s)/Violation(s): MURDER, CONSPIRACY TO MURDER, BOMBING
OF U.S. EMBASSIES

Name and Section(s) of Criminal Code: TITLE U.S. CODE 18, section
930B, 844F & 2332B

Maximum Penalty: LIFE

Time Left to Serve: Not Applicable

Facts of Case:

USAMA BIN LADEN CONSPIRED TO KILL U.S. NATIONALS THROUGH BOMBINGS OF

U.S. EMBASSIES IN KENYA AND TANZANIA ON AUGUST 7, 1998. IN ADDITION, SUBJECT IS ALSO WANTED FOR THE KILLING OF TWO GERMAN NATIONALS WHICH OCCURRED IN MARCH 1994 IN LIBYA AND IS THE SUBJECT OF AN INTERPOL RED NOTICE, FILE NO. 1998/20232, CONTROL NO. A-268/5-1998.

Additional Information:

THE U.S. GOVERNMENT HAS AUTHORIZED A $5 MILLION DOLLAR REWARD FOR INFORMATION LEADING TO THE LOCATION, ARREST AND CONVICTION OF THIS SUBJECT.

SPECIAL ATTENTION NCBS: PARIS, LONDON, RIYADH, CAIRO, MADRID, RABAT, ISTANBUL

SUBJECT HAS BEEN KNOWN TO TRAVEL TO AND THROUGH YOUR COUNTRIES. CHECK ALL ENTRY AND EXIT DATABASES FOR THE PRESENCE OF THE SUBJECT IN YOUR TERRITORIES AND ADVISE. PLEASE ALSO PLACE APPROPRIATE LOOKOUTS.

If your authorities can detain this fugitive under your laws pending receipt of a U.S. request for provisional arrest, please advise how long they can and will do so.

If, in lieu of extradition, your authorities can exclude, expel, deport, or otherwise remove this fugitive, please advise.

If this fugitive is located in a country that cannot extradite or otherwise remove the fugitive directly to the United States, please record his/her movements and immediately notify Interpol Washington and IPSG, citing our reference number above.

Regards
End - Interpol Washington

```
*******************************************************************************

FROM NCIC   ON 02/17/00 AT 11:56:29     PRESS ENTER TO CONTINUE
1L01CQUP0HX89000890
DCINTERT5

MKE/WANTED PERSON - CAUTION
ORI/NYFBINY03 NAM/LADEN,USAMA BIN SEX/M RAC/U POB/SB DOB/19570101
HGT/605 WGT/150 EYE/BR0 HAI/BLK
OFF/HOMICIDE
DOW/19990701 OCA/KFBD05765
MIS/A&D WILL EXTR ESCAPE RISK TERR0RIST C0NSP T0 MURDER US NATLS D0B HGT
MIS/WGTAPPR0X WLKS W/CANE SA C0LEMAN 265ANY259391 I49
ORI IS FBI NEW YORK 212 384-1000
AKA/ABDALLAH,ABU
AKA/BINLADEN,USAMAH BIN MUHAMMAD
AKA/BINLADEN,SHAYKH USAMAH
AKA/MUJAHIDSHAYKH,HAJI QAQA
AKA/PRINCE,THE
AKA/EMIR,THE
NIC/W920105315 DTE/19990824 1013 EDT
IMMED CONFIRM WARRANT AND EXTRADITION WITH ORI
```

Refer to FBI

FBI TEN MOST WANTED FUGITIVE

MURDER OF U.S. NATIONALS OUTSIDE THE UNITED STATES; CONSPIRACY TO MURDER U.S. NATIONALS OUTSIDE THE UNITED STATES; ATTACK ON A FEDERAL FACILITY RESULTING IN DEATH

USAMA BIN LADEN

Date of Photograph Unknown

Aliases: Usama Bin Muhammad Bin Ladin, Shaykh Usama Bin Ladin, the Prince, the Emir, Abu Abdallah, Mujahid Shaykh, Hajj, the Director

DESCRIPTION

Date of Birth:	1957	**Hair:**	Brown
Place of Birth:	Saudi Arabia	**Eyes:**	Brown
Height:	6' 4" to 6' 6"	**Complexion:**	Olive
Weight:	Approximately 160 pounds	**Sex:**	Male
Build:	Thin	**Nationality:**	Saudi Arabian
Occupations:	Unknown		
Remarks:	Leader of a terrorist organization known as Al-Qaeda "The Base". He walks with a cane.		
Scars and Marks:	None		

CAUTION

USAMA BIN LADEN IS WANTED IN CONNECTION WITH THE AUGUST 7,

1998, BOMBINGS OF THE UNITED STATES EMBASSIES IN DAR ES SALAAM, TANZANIA AND NAIROBI, KENYA. THESE ATTACKS KILLED OVER 200 PEOPLE.

CONSIDERED ARMED AND EXTREMELY DANGEROUS

IF YOU HAVE ANY INFORMATION CONCERNING THIS PERSON, PLEASE CONTACT YOUR LOCAL FBI OFFICE OR THE NEAREST U.S. EMBASSY OR CONSULATE.

REWARD

The United States Government is offering a reward of up to $5 million for information leading directly to the apprehension or conviction of Usama Bin Laden.

June 1999

[View PDF Version] [Ten Most Wanted Fugitives]
[Most Wanted Page] [Facts] [FBI Home Page]
[Hear The Soundbites] [U.S. Embassy Bombings] [New York Field Office]

Refer to FBI

PRIORITY: URGENT

DATE: 04 Dec 1998

FROM: Interpol Washington

TO: [redacted] b7D   INTERPOL - USNCB

CC: Investigating Agency: FBI
              Prosecuting Agency: U.S. ATTORNEY'S OFFICE
              Office of International Affairs, US Department of Justice

OUR REF: [redacted] b2, b7C   INTERPOL - USNCB

YOUR REF: New Inquiry

REGARDING: Fugitive Broadcast - BIN LADEN, F/N USAMA

ASF: No Exclusions

On behalf of the FBI please locate the following fugitive and immediately notify
Interpol Washington and IPSG. Upon notification, U.S. authorities will, if
possible, formally request provisional arrest with a view toward extradition in
accordance with any applicable extradition treaty.

Present Family Name: BIN LADEN

Family Name at Birth: BIN LADEN

First Name: USAMA

Date of Birth: 1957

Approximate Age: 41

Place of Birth: JEDDAH, SAUDI ARABIA

Nationality(ies): SAUDI ARABIAN

Alias(es):
          USAMA BIN LADEN, AKA
          USAMAH BIN-MUHAMMAD BIN-LADIN
          SHAYKH USAMA BIN-LADIN
          ABU ABDULLAH
          MUJAHID SHAYKH
          HAJJ

Name of Father: BIN LADEN, ABDUL RAHAMN AWADH

Name of Mother: NOT AVAILABLE   INTERPOL - USNCB

Refer to FBI

Skin Tone: Olive

Height: 195.58 CM / 6 FT 5 IN

Weight: 61.376 KG / 137 POUNDS

Eye Color: Brown

Hair Color: Brown

Physical Descriptors: FULL BEARD, MUSTACHE, WALKS WITH CANE

Language(s) Spoken: ARABIC

Occupation: RELIGIOUS CLERIC; ARMS DEALER

Areas likely to be visited: MIDDLE EAST, WESTERN EUROPE

Passport: NOT AVAILABLE

Misc. ID: NOT AVAILABLE

Fingerprints: Not Available

Photograph: Attached

Caution/Warning:
        ARMED AND DANGEROUS

Arrest Warrant Number: S(2)98CR.1023

Arrest Date: 04 NOV 1998

By (Judge): JAMES M. PARKISON, U.S. DISTRICT COURT SOUTHERN DISTRICT OF NEW YORK

City and State: NEW YORK, NEW YORK

Name of Offense(s)/Violation(s): MURDER, CONSPIRACY TO MURDER, BOMBING OF U.S. EMBASSIES

Name and Section(s) of Criminal Code: TITLE U.S. CODE 18, section 930B, 844F & 2332B

Maximum Penalty: LIFE

Time Left to Serve: Not Applicable

Facts of Case:

USAMA BIN LADEN CONSPIRED TO KILL U.S. NATIONALS THROUGH BOMBINGS OF U.S. EMBASSIES IN KENYA AND TANZANIA ON AUGUST 7, 1998. IN ADDITION, SUBJECT IS ALSO WANTED FOR THE KILLING OF TWO GERMAN NATIONALS WHICH OCCURRED IN MARCH 1994 IN LIBYA AND IS THE SUBJECT OF AN INTERPOL RED NOTICE, FILE NO. 1998/20232, CONTROL NO. A-268/5-1998.

Refer to FBI

PRIORITY: Normal

DATE: 23 February 2000

FROM: Interpol Washington

TO: [redacted] b2, b7C

OUR REF: [redacted]

SUBJECT: Wanted Person Diffusion Bin Laden, f/n Usama born in 1957

RedHead   PERSON WANTED FOR PROSECUTION

1.   IDENTITY PARTICULARS

WARNING: THIS PERSON MAY BE:
        Armed
        Dangerous

1.1   PRESENT FAMILY NAME:
       Bin Laden

1.2   FAMILY NAME AT BIRTH / PREVIOUS FAMILY NAMES:
       Bin Laden

1.3   FORENAMES:
       Usama,

1.4   SEX:
       M

1.5   DATE AND PLACE OF BIRTH:
       Date Unknown, 1957
       Jeddah,
       Saudi Arabia

1.6   FATHER'S FAMILY NAME AND FORENAMES:
       Bin Laden, Abdul Rahamn Awadh

1.7   MOTHER'S MAIDEN NAME AND FORENAMES:
       not known,

1.8   RESULT OF IDENTITY CHECK:
       IDENTITY CONFIRMED

1.9   NATIONALITY(IES):
       Saudi Arabia ...   (CONFIRMED)

1.10   IDENTITY DOCUMENTS:
       Passport Number: not known
       Other Identification Information:

Refer to FBI

PRIORITY: Normal

DATE: 23 February 2000

FROM: Interpol Washington

TO: ████████████ b2, b7C **INTERPOL - USNCB**

OUR REF: ████████████

SUBJECT: Wanted Person Diffusion Bin Laden, f/n Usama born in 1957

On Behalf of the Federal Bureau of Investigation please locate the following fugitive and immediately notify Interpol Washington and the IPSG. Upon notification, U.S. authorities will, if possible, formally request provisional arrest with a view toward extradition in accordance with any applicable extradition treaty.

If your authorities can detain this fugitive under your laws pending a receipt of a U.S. request for provisional arrest, please advise how long they can and will do so.

If, in lieu of extradition, your authorities can exclude, expel, deport, or otherwise remove this fugitive, please advise.

If this fugitive is located in a country that cannot extradite or otherwise remove the fugitive directly to the United States, please record his/her movements and immediately notify Interpol Washington and IPSG, citing our reference number above.

1.   IDENTITY PARTICULARS

WARNING: THIS PERSON MAY BE:
        Armed
        Dangerous

1.1   PRESENT FAMILY NAME:
      Bin Laden

1.2   FAMILY NAME AT BIRTH / PREVIOUS FAMILY NAMES:
      Bin Laden

1.3   FORENAMES:
      Usama,

1.4   SEX:
      M

1.5   DATE AND PLACE OF BIRTH:
      Date Unknown, 1957
      Jeddah,
      Saudi Arabia

1.6   FATHER'S FAMILY NAME AND FORENAMES:

Refer to FBI

From: [████] b7C
Sent: Monday, December 13, 1999 9:20 AM
To: [████] b7C
Subject: FW: CONTINUED USAMA BIN LADEN-RELATED THREATS

[████]-SEE ME-[████] b7C   **INTERPOL - USNCB**
-----Original Message-----
From: [████]
Sent: Saturday, December 11, 1999 1:53 PM
To: USNCB State Group [████]
Cc: [████]
Subject: CONTINUED USAMA BIN LADEN-RELATED THREATS

JNLET
0022 13:24:41 12/11/99
*OO LL JIPOL .

AM.DCFBIWAD8
11:16 12/11/99 01175
11:16 12/11/99 00278 DJ

TXT
(AP)
REQUEST NATIONAL BROADCAST
ML0114702 KLANQUIST

CONTINUED USAMA BIN LADEN-RELATED THREATS
  THIS IS NOT A TERRORIST THREAT ALERT OR ADVISORY; IT
IS FOR INFORMATION PURPOSES ONLY.
  ALTHOUGH UNCLASSIFIED, THIS COMMUNICATION SHOULD BE
HANDLED AS LAW ENFORCEMENT SENSITIVE. THIS
COMMUNICATION SHOULD NOT BE FURNISHED TO THE MEDIA OR
OTHER AGENCIES OUTSIDE THE LAW ENFORCEMENT/U.S.
GOVERNMENT COUNTERTERRORISM COMMUNITY WITHOUT THE
PERMISSION OF THE FBI. UNAUTHORIZED DISCLOSURE OF FBI
COMMUNICATIONS COULD JEOPARDIZE ONGOING FBI
INVESTIGATIONS.
END PART 1 OF 5

THE FBI CONTINUES TO RECEIVE THREATS FROM INDIVIDUALS AND ORGANIZATIONS WITH TIES TO USAMA
BIN LADEN AND HIS ORGANIZATION, AL-QAEDA. SEVERAL FACTORS HEIGHTEN THE POTENTIAL FOR
TERRORISM WITHIN THE UNITED STATES. THESE INCLUDE THE CONTINUED LARGE NUMBER OF THREATS
RECEIVED, THE INDICTMENT AGAINST BIN LADEN, HIS ADDITION TO THE FBI'S "TEN MOST WANTED
FUGITIVES" LIST, THE ONGOING U.S. INVESTIGATION AND SEARCH FOR BIN LADEN, THE UPCOMING TRIAL
OF BIN LADEN ASSOCIATES IN THE SOUTHERN DISTRICT OF NEW YORK, AND THE PERCEIVED
SIGNIFICANCE OF THE YEAR 2000. END PART 2 OF 5

AS RECIPIENTS ARE AWARE, SIX INDIVIDUALS ASSOCIATED WITH BIN LADEN ARE CURRENTLY AWAITING
TRIAL IN THE SOUTHERN DISTRICT OF NEW YORK IN CONNECTION WITH THEIR ROLES IN THE EAST AFRICA
EMBASSY BOMBINGS. THEY FACE NUMEROUS CHARGES, INCLUDING CONSPIRACY TO MURDER U.S.
CITIZENS AND EFFORTS TO OBTAIN CHEMICAL AND BIOLOGICAL WEAPONS. THE PRE-TRIAL PROCESS FOR
THESE INDIVIDUALS IS SCHEDULED TO BEGIN IN JANUARY 2000. AN ADDITIONAL THREE INDIVIDUALS ARE
IN CUSTODY IN THE UNITED KINGDOM FACING EXTRADITION TO THE UNITED STATES, AND EIGHT
ADDITIONAL FUGITIVES ARE BEING VIGOROUSLY PURSUED WORLDWIDE. END PART 3 OF 5

IN ADDITION, THE PERIOD OF TIME LEADING UP TO AND THROUGH THE NEW YEAR AND RAMADAN POSES
DISTINCT COUNTERTERRORISM CHALLENGES. IN THE UNITED STATES, SOME VIOLENT EXTREMISTS
ATTACH SPECIAL SIGNIFICANCE TO THE YEAR 2000. RELIGIOUS MOTIVATION AND POLITICAL IDEOLOGY
(SUCH AS THE NEW WORLD ORDER CONSPIRACY THEORY) MAY LEAD EXTREMIST GROUPS OR INDIVIDUALS
TO TAKE VIOLENT ACTION AT YEAR'S END. SOME INTERNATIONAL TERRORISTS, SUCH AS USAMA BIN
LADEN AND HIS ORGANIZATION, AL-QAEDA, MAY ALSO FOCUS ON THE NEW YEAR AS A BACKDROP FOR
VIOLENT ATTACKS AGAINST U.S. INTERESTS. PART 4 OF 5

  THE FBI POSSESSES NO SPECIFIC INFORMATION AT THIS TIME INDICATING THAT ANY TERRORIST GROUPS
OR INDIVIDUALS ARE PLANNING ATTACKS WITHIN THE UNITED STATES. RECIPIENTS ARE ENCOURAGED TO

REMAIN VIGILANT AND ALEF[ ] [ ]OSSIBLE ACTS OF TERRORISM / [ ] [ ]EPORT ANY INFORMATION THI[ ]Y MAY DEVELOP PERTAININ[ ] [ ]THIS MATTER TO THEIR LOCAL [ ]BI [ ]FICE OR FBI HEADQUARTERS.
END PART 5 OF 5 END TRANSMISSION

NLETS Message   NLETS Message   NLETS Message   NLETS Message   NLETS Message

INTERPOL - USNCB

FEDERAL BUREAU OF INVESTIGATION
FOI/PA
DELETED PAGE INFORMATION SHEET
FOI/PA# 1165436-0

Total Deleted Page(s) = 3
Page 52 ~ Referral/Direct;
Page 53 ~ Referral/Direct;
Page 54 ~ Referral/Direct;

```
XXXXXXXXXXXXXXXXXXXXXXX
X    Deleted Page(s)     X
X    No Duplication Fee X
X    For this Page      X
XXXXXXXXXXXXXXXXXXXXXXX
```

FEDERAL BUREAU OF INVESTIGATION

Precedence: IMMEDIATE   Date: 10/05/2000

To: All Field Offices   Attn: ADIC;
                                           SAC
     All Legats   Attn: Legat
     National Security   Attn: SSA [   ]

From: New York
          Squad [   ]
          Contact: SA [   ]

Approved By: [   ]

Drafted By: [   ]

Case ID #: [   ] (Pending)   b6
           [   ] (~~Pending~~)   b7A
                                                    b7C
                                                    b7E
                                                    b3

Title: USAMA BIN LADEN
        MAJOR CASE #161

        AL-QAEDA;
        THE ISLAMIC ARMY;
        OO:NY

Synopsis: The purpose of this communication is advise all field
offices to allow access in ACS to [   ] case files related to UBL
to NYO and reiterate reporting guidelines for information being
routed to New York for the above referenced case files.

Details: It has recently come to the attention of NYO that other
field offices have not opened access to Usama Bin Laden/Al Qaeda
related [   ] cases. Many field offices have access through ACS to
NYO's files, but NYO has been unable to access through ACS
related cases in other field offices. It is therefore requested
that all field offices with [   ] cases relating to UBL/Al-Qaeda,
allow access to those files to the following NYO personnel:

          SSA [   ]   b6
          SA [   ] and   b7C
          [   ]

          For information of receiving offices, the Kenbom/Tanbom
trial is scheduled to begin January 3, 2001 for the following six
defendants currently in custody:

          Wadih El-Hage;
          Ali Mohamed;
          Mamdouh Mahmud Salim;
          Mohamed Sadeek Odeh;
          Mohamed Rashed Daoud Al-'Owhali; and

Khalfan Khamis Mohamed

The indictment alleges the defendants conspired to murder, bomb and maim. Specifically, the defendants were part of an international terrorist group dedicated to opposing non-Islamic governments with force and violence. The group calling itself "AL-QAEDA" was formed by defendants UBL and Muhammad Atef and others. It was a part and an object of said conspiracy that the defendants, and others known and unknown would and did murder United States nationals anywhere in the world. In furtherance of said conspiracy, and to effect the illegal objects thereof, the following overt acts, among others were committed:

Guesthouses and training camps for Al-Qaeda and its affiliated groups were established. American citizens were recruited in order to utilize the American citizens for travel. Surveillance of embassies took place. Financial dealings took place on behalf of Al-Qaeda, including, but not limited to: purchasing land for training camps; purchasing explosives; purchasing communication equipment; and transporting currency and weapons to members of Al-Qaeda worldwide.

Due to the large amount of documents being generated in the above referenced case files and the variety of classification levels involved, New York is requesting all offices proceed under the following guidelines when generating paperwork on these matters.

The [   ] file is the criminal portion of the USAMA BIN LADEN investigation and any requests/responses for toll records, financial records or other subpoenas and other leads should be UNCLASSIFIED. Responses to leads should be contained on FD-302s, inserts or other appropriate documentation and forwarded in an unclassified manner. If the response/request contains information that should by its nature, be classified, it should be directed to [   ]. In addition, it is requested that all responses to New York contain the appropriate sub-file, which are referenced in the outgoing communication sent by NYO setting the lead. FD 302's should contain file # [   ] for direct uploading in ACS under the [   ] file. Additionally, [   ] requested under the criminal case. New York will provide subpoenas for obtaining such information. No [   ] derived material should be sent to this file unless it has been cleared for passage to the criminal case.

b1
b3
b7A
b7E

(S)

Numerous subfiles have been opened on various subjects,

searches, etc, and are designated on outgoing communications.
Receiving offices are requested to respond to leads under these
designated subfiles.

        If an investigation is opened as an intelligence matter
related to the [____] AL-QAEDA file, or results in another
division opening an intelligence case based on information
provided by New York, communications to New York should be
directed to [_____] not the [_____] case. Any
[____] derived material should not be sent to the [__] file. [____]
derived intelligence related to BIN LADEN should be provided
under the [__] caption only.

        New York requests compliance of the above to facilitate
disclosure obligations, maximize the results of investigative
efforts for criminal use and prosecution and minimize the
likelihood of unwanted disclosures which could compromise
sensitive techniques of intelligence.

FEDERAL BUREAU OF INVESTIGATION

Precedence: ROUTINE   Date: 10/13/2000

To: Los Angeles   Attn: Resident Agency IT Supervisors

From: Los Angeles
     NSD-4
     Contact: SA

Approved By:

Drafted By

Case ID #: (X)   (Pending)

Title: (X) AL-QAEDA;
     THE ISLAMIC ARMY;
     OO:NY

Synopsis: (X) All Resident Agencies are requested to provide to
NSD-4 a list of all current UBL-related [   ] matters and ensure
that ACS access to those files is provided to the named
individuals below.

(U) (X)   Derived From: G-3
        Declassify On: X1

Reference:

Details: (X) Pursuant to the referenced EC, FBI New York has
notified all field offices that FBI New York does not have ACS
access to USAMA BIN LADEN/AL-QAEDA-related [   ] cases. FBI New
York has set leads requesting that each field office, with
current [   ] cases relating to USAMA BIN LADEN/AL-QAEDA, allow ACS
access to the following FBI New York personnel:

    SSA
    SA   b6
                                    b7C

(U) (X) Access to these cases is necessary in order to
assist in the preparation for trial of six defendants in the
Kenbom/Tanbom criminal investigation.

OCT 2 4

        (U) (⊠)   Accordingly, each Resident Agency is requested to
review all current [____] matters relating to USAMA BIN LADEN/AL-
QAEDA and provide a list of those case titles and file numbers to
SA [_____] NSD-4. Each Resident Agency is requested to
ensure that any files with ACS restricted access are modified to
allow access to the named FBI New York Personnel. Additionally,
on the list, please indicate whether each file was previously
"access-restricted." Resident Agencies with no such cases are
requested to respond as well, stating so. Upon receipt of
responses from all Resident Agencies, SA [____] will respond to
FBI New York covering the lead set by [_____]

LEAD(s):

Set Lead 1:

LOS ANGELES

AT LOS ANGELES INTERNATIONAL AIRPORT, CALIFORNIA

(U) (X) Each Resident Agency (RA) Supervisor with NFIP/IT Program management responsibility is requested to review all current [____] (USAMA BIN LADEN/AL-QAEDA) investigations to determine whether or not those cases had restricted access. Supervisors are also requested to modify any restricted access (199N) investigations to ensure New York personnel described in instant text have access. It is further requested that a response (affirmative or negative) be provided to SA [_____] [____] NSD-4, so that an appropriate division response is forwarded to New York Division in a timely matter.

Set Lead 2:

LOS ANGELES

AT LANCASTER, CALIFORNIA

(U) (X) Each Resident Agency (RA) Supervisor with NFIP/IT Program management responsibility is requested to review all current [____] (USAMA BIN LADEN/AL-QAEDA) investigations to determine whether or not those cases had restricted access. Supervisors are also requested to modify any restricted access [____] investigations to ensure New York personnel described in instant text have access. It is further requested that a response (affirmative or negative) be provided to SA [_____] [____] NSD-4, so that an appropriate division response is forwarded to New York Division in a timely matter.

Set Lead 3:

LOS ANGELES

AT LONG BEACH, CALIFORNIA

(U) (X) Each Resident Agency (RA) Supervisor with NFIP/IT Program management responsibility is requested to review all current [____] (USAMA BIN LADEN/AL-QAEDA) investigations to

determine whether or not those cases had restricted access.
Supervisors are also requested to modify any restricted access
[ ] investigations to ensure New York personnel described in
instant text have access. It is further requested that a
response (affirmative or negative) be provided to SA [ ]
[ ] NSD-4, so that an appropriate division response is
forwarded to New York Division in a timely matter.

Set Lead 4:

   LOS ANGELES

      AT PALM SPRINGS, CALIFORNIA

   (U)   (S)   Each Resident Agency (RA) Supervisor with NFIP/IT
Program management responsibility is requested to review all
current [ ] (USAMA BIN LADEN/AL-QAEDA) investigations to
determine whether or not those cases had restricted access.
Supervisors are also requested to modify any restricted access
[ ] investigations to ensure New York personnel described in
instant text have access. It is further requested that a
response (affirmative or negative) be provided to SA [ ]
[ ] NSD-4, so that an appropriate division response is
forwarded to New York Division in a timely matter.

Set Lead 5:

   LOS ANGELES

      AT RIVERSIDE, CALIFORNIA

   (U)   (S)   Each Resident Agency (RA) Supervisor with NFIP/IT
Program management responsibility is requested to review all
current [ ] (USAMA BIN LADEN/AL-QAEDA) investigations to
determine whether or not those cases had restricted access.
Supervisors are also requested to modify any restricted access
[ ] investigations to ensure New York personnel described in
instant text have access. It is further requested that a
response (affirmative or negative) be provided to SA [ ]
[ ] NSD-4, so that an appropriate division response is
forwarded to New York Division in a timely matter.

Set Lead 6:

   LOS ANGELES

AT SANTA ANA, CALIFORNIA

(U) (☒)   Each Resident Agency (RA) Supervisor with NFIP/IT Program management responsibility is requested to review all current [   ] (USAMA BIN LADEN/AL-QAEDA) investigations to determine whether or not those cases had restricted access. Supervisors are also requested to modify any restricted access [   ] investigations to ensure New York personnel described in instant text have access. It is further requested that a response (affirmative or negative) be provided to SA [   ] [   ] NSD-4, so that an appropriate division response is forwarded to New York Division in a timely matter.

Set Lead 7:

LOS ANGELES

AT SANTA MARIA, CALIFORNIA

(U) (☒)   Each Resident Agency (RA) Supervisor with NFIP/IT Program management responsibility is requested to review all current [   ] (USAMA BIN LADEN/AL-QAEDA) investigations to determine whether or not those cases had restricted access. Supervisors are also requested to modify any restricted access [   ] investigations to ensure New York personnel described in instant text have access. It is further requested that a response (affirmative or negative) be provided to SA [   ] [   ] NSD-4, so that an appropriate division response is forwarded to New York Division in a timely matter.

Set Lead 8:

LOS ANGELES

AT VENTURA, CALIFORNIA

(U) (☒)   Each Resident Agency (RA) Supervisor with NFIP/IT Program management responsibility is requested to review all current [   ] (USAMA BIN LADEN/AL-QAEDA) investigations to determine whether or not those cases had restricted access. Supervisors are also requested to modify any restricted access [   ] investigations to ensure New York personnel described in instant text have access. It is further requested that a response (affirmative or negative) be provided to SA [   ] [   ] NSD-4, so that an appropriate division response is forwarded to New York Division in a timely matter.

Set Lead 9:

<u>LOS ANGELES</u>

AT VICTORVILLE, CALIFORNIA

(U) (S)   Each Resident Agency (RA) Supervisor with NFIP/IT Program management responsibility is requested to review all current [_____] (USAMA BIN LADEN/AL-QAEDA) investigations to determine whether or not those cases had restricted access. Supervisors are also requested to modify any restricted access [_____] investigations to ensure New York personnel described in instant text have access. It is further requested that a response (affirmative or negative) be provided to SA [_____] [_____] NSD-4, so that an appropriate division response is forwarded to New York Division in a timely matter.

b6
b7C
b7E

Set Lead 10:

<u>LOS ANGELES</u>

AT WEST COVINA, CALIFORNIA

(U) (S)   Each Resident Agency (RA) Supervisor with NFIP/IT Program management responsibility is requested to review all current [_____] (USAMA BIN LADEN/AL-QAEDA) investigations to determine whether or not those cases had restricted access. Supervisors are also requested to modify any restricted access [_____] investigations to ensure New York personnel described in instant text have access. It is further requested that a response (affirmative or negative) be provided to SA [_____] [_____] NSD-4, so that an appropriate division response is forwarded to New York Division in a timely matter.

♦♦

(U) To: Counterterrorism From: Sacramento
Re: (X) [ ] 11/02/2000

LEAD(S):

Set Lead 1:

COUNTERTERRORISM

AT WASHINGTON, D.C.

(X) IOS [ ] is requested to review the enclosed information. SC T-1 is scheduled to travel approximately 12/15/2000. Should SC T-1 be of interest and CT has any tasking, (S) it is requested CT provide tasking to SC [ ] (S) [ ]

Set Lead 2:

NEW YORK

AT NEW YORK CITY, NEW YORK

(U) (X) NY is requested to review and advise SC if SC T-1 is in a position to be tasked by NY.

Set Lead 3:

SACRAMENTO

AT SACRAMENTO, CALIFORNIA

(U) (X) Should CT provide a positive response and request tasking, SA [ ] is requested to obtain appropriate SAC SC approval to operate as an "Operational Asset" (OA).

♦♦

FEDERAL BUREAU OF INVESTIGATION

Precedence: ROUTINE   **Date:** 11/03/2000

To: New York   **Attn:**
                                              SA

From: Albuquerque
          Squad
          Contact: SA   b6
                                                                 b7C
          oved By: b7E

Drafted By:

Case ID #: (U)   (Pending)
                                                b7E
Title: (U)   AL-QAEDA   b3
                 THE ISLAMIC ARMY
                 OO:NY

Synopsis: (U) Lead covered. New York Office personnel have
been granted access to the Albuquerque Division's pending
files.

          (U) (S)   **Derived From :** G-3
                          Declassify On: X1

Reference: (U)   b7A

(U) **Details:** (S) In the referenced communication, the New York
Office set a lead for receiving offices to allow SSA
                                              access to all
          cases relating to Usama Bin Laden/Al-Qaeda. Based on this
request, the Albuquerque Division has granted access to the
following pending classified   files

          (U) Albuquerque considers the lead covered.

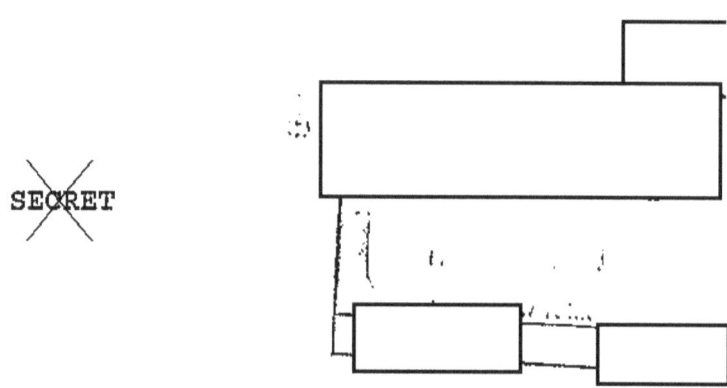

FEDERAL BUREAU OF INVESTIGATION

Precedence: IMMEDIATE   **Date:** 11/09/2000

To: ✓New York   **Attn:** ✓Squad ▢
                                              SA ▢

From: Las Vega▢
         Squad
         Conta▢ IRS▢

Approved B▢

Drafted By▢

Case ID #: (S) ▢ (Pending) ▢   b7A
            (U) (S) ▢ (Pending) ▢   b7E
            (S) ▢ (Pending) ▢   b3

(U) **Title:** (S) USAMA BIN LADEN;
                    MAJOR CASE 3161

                    AL-QAEDA;
                    THE ISLAMIC ARMY

(U) **Synopsis:** (S) To provide Federal Bureau of Investigation (FBI)
New York access through the Automated Case Support system (ACS)
to FBI ▢ investigation.

(U) (S)   **Derived From :** G-3
           Declassify On: X-1

(U) **Reference:** (S) ▢   b7A
                   (S) ▢

(U) **Details:** (S) Referenced communications advised that it has
recently come to the attention of FBI New York, that other field
offices have not opened access to Usama Bin Laden (UBL)/Al-Qaeda
related ▢ cases. Many field offices have access through ACS to
FBI New York files, but FBI New York has been unable to access
through ACS related cases in other field offices. FBI New York
requested that field offices with ▢ cases relating to
UBL/Al-Qaeda, allow access to those files to the following FBI
New York personnel:

SEARCHED _____ INDEXED _____   b6
SERIALIZED _____ FILED _____   b7
                                    b7

NOV

To: New York   From: Las Vegas
(U) Re: (S) [_____] 11/09/2000   b7A

        SSA [_____]
        SA [_____] ; and
        [_____]

    (U) (S)   On 11/07/2000, Information Management Assistant
(IMA) [_____], FBI Las Vegas, assigned a special
role to above listed FBI New York personnel, thus allowing them
access to [_____] through ACS.

        (U)   Las Vegas considers this lead covered.

CC: IRS [_____]

♦♦

FEDERAL BUREAU OF INVESTIGATION

Precedence: PRIORITY   Date: 11/29/2000

To: Counterterrorism Division   Attn: [   ]/SIOC/CAT A/B, 5328

From: San Diego
        Squad [   ]
        Contact:

Approved By:

Drafted By:

(U) Case ID #: (S) [   ] (Pending)

(U) Title: (S) USAMA BIN LADEN/AL-QAEDA
              IT-UBL/AL-QAEDA
              OO: NY

(U) Synopsis: (S) Advising lead covered in referenced EC.

        (U) (S)   Derived From : G-3
                        Declassify On: X1

(U) Reference: (S) [   ]

(U) Details: (S) Normal intelligence and threat assessment
protocols continue at San Diego Division through the Joint
Terrorism Task Force and the San Diego Anti-Terrorism Team which
includes the Immigration and Naturalization Service, U.S. Border
Patrol, and the United States Customs Service. Additionally, San
Diego advised all agents in the division via E-mail to report any
related threat information to FBIHQ.

        (U) (S) San Diego considers this lead covered as no further
investigation remains.

LEAD/ASSIGN/COVERED
DATE
ASSIGN TO
SUPV   SECRET

SERIALIZED

DEC 5 2000

b6
b7

FEDERAL BUREAU OF INVESTIGATION

Precedence: IMMEDIATE   Date: 11/15/2000

To: National Security   Attn: SSA [   ]
     New York   SA [   ]

From: Los Angeles
      NSD-4
      Contact: SA [   ]

Approved By [   ]

Drafted By: [   ]

(U) Case ID #: (S) [   ] (Pending)

(U) Title: (S)   AL-QAEDA;
                    THE ISLAMIC ARMY;
                    OO:NY

(U) Synopsis: (S)   Cover lead set by New York and provide ACS access
     to [   ] cases relating to UBL/Al-Qaeda to specified New York
     personnel.

             (U) (S) b7E   Derived From : G-3
                       b3   Declassify On: X1

     Reference: [   ]

(U) Details: (S)   By way of referenced serial, FBI New York
     requested that FBI Los Angeles review all current [   ] cases
     related to Usama Bin Laden/Al-Qaeda and provide ACS access to
     these cases to SSA [   ] and [ ]
     [   ]

             (U) (S)   FBI Los Angeles has reviewed its files and has
     determined that the following files are currently pending and
     relate to UBL/Al-Qaeda:

                                          b6
                                          b7C
                                          b7E
                                          b3

LEAD/ASSIGO/COVERED
DATE
ASSIGN TO
SUPV

SECRET

SERIALIZED_____ FILED_____

DEC 05 2000

To: National Security From: Los Angeles
(U) Re: (X) [   ] 11/15/2000

    (U) (S) FBI Los Angeles has ensured that ACS access has been granted to the specified New York personnel. FBI Los Angeles considers this lead covered.

pls mark lead
covered.
↓ Tht
Lead Covered
11-24-00
/11-21-00

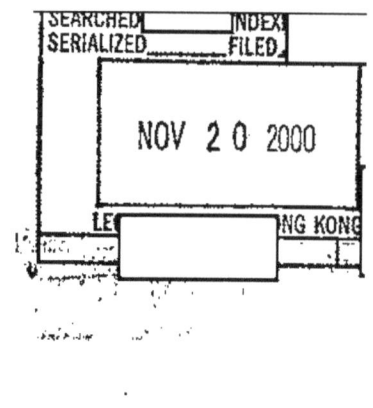

Precedence: PRIORITY   Date: 11/14/2000

To: All Field Offices   Attn: SACs

    All Legats   Attn: LEGATs

From: Counterterrorism Division   b7E
    [   ] SIOC/CAT A/B, 5328
      Contact: Unit Chief [   ]
             Unit Chief

Approved By: b6
                                                 b7C

Drafted By:

Case ID #: (S) [   ] (Pending)

Title: (S) USAMA BIN LADEN/AL-QAEDA
         IT-UBL/AL-QAEDA
         OO: NY

Synopsis: (S/NF)   This communication provides recipients with
information relative to the potential for terrorist activity inside
the United States by terrorists operating within Al-Qaeda and the
international jihad movement. In addition, this communication requests
that recipients ensure that information relating to any potential acts
of terrorist violence be disseminated on a timely basis to FBI
Headquarters for appropriate action. Finally, those offices with
border responsibilities and international airports are requested to
review procedures with appropriate officials of the U.S. Immigration
and Naturalization Service (INS), U.S. Customs Service (USCS) and
other law enforcement entities.

  (U) (S)   Classified By: 4877, NS3/CTD
              Reason   : 1.5(c)
              Declassify On: X1

Details: (S/OC/NF)   There have been claims of responsibility by four
(4) groups regarding the October 12, 2000, attack on the USS Cole.
Those groups include the Islamic Army of Aden, Islamic Deterrent
Forces, Mohammad's Army and the Organization of the Oppressed in Jabal

----

Case ID [   ]

Amil. Like previous suspected Usama Bin Laden-sponsored attacks in East Africa in 1998, and planned attacks in Jordan in 1999, the United States was the intended target for an attack designed to bring about the deaths of American citizens. In totality, two hundred and forty-one (241) persons, including 31 Americans, were killed in the terrorist bombings in Kenya and Yemen.

(U) In addition to targeting U.S. interests overseas, terrorists operating in support of the international jihad movement have also conducted acts of terrorism on U.S. soil. Specifically, on February 26, 1993, Islamic extremists of various nationalities aligned with Sheikh Omar Abdel Rahman, spiritual leader of the Egyptian Al Gama Al Islamiyya (AGAI) and the Egyptian Islamic Jihad (EIJ), bombed the World Trade Center (WTC) in New York City. Six persons were killed and another 1,000 were injured in this attack. Subsequent to this attack, the FBI thwarted a plot in June 1993 by other Islamic extremists operating under the guidance of Sheikh Rahman to bomb several targets in the New York metropolitan area. Prior to this time, the United States appeared invulnerable to international terrorist activity on U.S. soil.

(U) (S/NF) In addition, the FBI investigation regarding Ahmed Ressam and his attempt to enter the United States in December, 1999, continues. As receiving offices are aware, on December 14, 1999, Ressam was arrested after attempting to enter the United States at the Port Angeles, Washington, point of entry. Ressam, who was carrying multiple forms of identification in varying names, was transporting items which could be used to make several explosive devices. To date, Ressam's target(s) in the United States are unknown. It is also unknown how many others were involved in the plot, and the organizational structure of the group of individuals associated with this case. In addition, it is unknown if Ressam was acting on behalf of a specific terrorist group/sponsor. Ressam and some of his conspirators have been linked to the overall Sunni Islamic extremists network.

(U) (S/NF) Guided by radical spiritual leaders, such as Sheikh Rahman, and extremist Islamic benefactors, such as UBL, terrorist attacks conducted by the international jihad movement are increasingly overshadowing attacks conducted by other terrorist groups and state sponsors. Further, the level of sophistication and lethality of attacks has significantly increased over the years. This is believed to be attributed to the conjoin of former Arab-Afghan mujahadeen with extensive explosives and combat experience into a movement dedicated to international jihad. The well-planned attack on the USS Cole, a U.S. Navy destroyer, is indicative of the capabilities and impudence of this movement and its members/supporters.

(U) (S/NF) In response to the attack on the USS Cole and the continuing threat posed by UBL and other terrorists operating within the framework of the international jihad movement, a number of disruption operations have been initiated overseas. Intelligence gleaned, thus far, from these operations indicates that the United States continues to be a primary target for attack by UBL and his supporters. In addition, intelligence suggests that there may be plans for additional attacks targeting U.S. interests. To date, however, the FBI is not in receipt of any specific target, location or time frame for reported UBL-supported attack(s). Nevertheless, disruption operations in the past have resulted in terrorist reprisals. As an example, in October 1995, the AGAI claimed responsibility for the suicide car bombing of local police headquarters in Rijeka, Croatia. This attack was in response to the detainment of an AGAI leader in Croatia. Further, in mid-November 1999, the FBI received information indicating that a Yemen-based UBL-aligned terrorist and unidentified terrorists residing in Pakistan had made plans to bomb U.S. targets in Saudi Arabia and Yemen. No specific U.S. targets were mentioned. The attacks, which ultimately were not carried out, were reportedly planned to retaliate for the execution of a Sunni extremist leader in Yemen.

(U) (S/NF) In addition to the potential threat posed by UBL and the international jihad movement, events currently unfolding in the world arena, such as the ongoing crisis in the Middle East, could portend potential acts of anti-U.S. terrorism by other Islamic extremists. Recently, the FBI learned that Egyptian AGAI leader [   ] [   ] who perceives the United States as pro-Israel, has called upon Islamic extremists worldwide to target American and Israeli interests. Specifically, on September 13, 2000, [   ] supra, issued a statement calling for Muslims to "liberate" Jerusalem, while at the same time, threatened U.S. interests in the Middle East. In the statement, [   ] clearly voiced his opposition to the "sharing of Jerusalem with Israel" and stated "we reject the possibility of giving up one inch of Muslim Palestine, to say nothing of Jerusalem." [   ] went on to say, "the United States must realize that the idolatrous paper-thin regime of the region will not be able to protect themselves from the anger of our people." "They must also realize that no one will be able to protect their interests in the region as long as they continue their double standards." [   ] concluded his statement with "raining down painful blows on Jews and Americans must constitute one of the most important religious duties for every able Muslim." In addition, intelligence indicates that the Jerusalem issue is paramount to UBL supporters because it signifies the Americans are crusaders.

(U) (S/NF) Further exacerbating the potential terrorist threat in the near term is the advent of Ramadan, the Muslim holy month of fasting, which begins circa November 27, 2000 and ends in late December 2000. In the past, Islamic extremists have engaged in violent acts of terrorism during this time period, particularly on the "Night of Power." According to Muslim tradition, "Laylatul Qadr" or the Night of Power, aka the Night of Destiny, represents the date when Allah first revealed the Quran to Muhammad. Also, on this night the gates of heaven are said to be open, sins are forgiven and prayers are answered for all those who pray. (Note: Muslim tradition dictates that the "Night of Power" occurs during the last ten days of Ramadan. During 1999, Ramadan was observed December 9, 1999 through January 7, 2000 and the Night of Power is believed to have been observed on January 4, 2000.) The "Night of Power" this year could fall on/about December 25, 2000.

(U) (S/NF) In order to adequately address the potential threat emanating from UBL/Al Qaeda and the international jihad movement, recipients are requested to provide FBIHQ with any threat-related information developed in your respective offices. In furtherance of this effort, field offices should task assets for any available information specifically relating to potential terrorist activity. In addition, those field offices with border responsibilities and international airports are requested to review procedures with appropriate officials of the INS, USCS, and other law enforcement entities.

(U) (S/NF) To reiterate, FBIHQ is currently not in receipt of any specific information to indicate that a UBL/Al Qaeda terrorist attack is imminent. However, given the present state of global affairs and intelligence indicating the United States remains a primary target for UBL and other Islamic extremists, the potential for anti-U.S. terrorist activity exists. Further, upcoming special events that afford widespread media coverage, particularly the Presidential Inauguration and the Super Bowl, could be attractive targets for such activity. You will be advised of additional information as it becomes available.

(U) Questions regarding this communication should be directed to Unit Chief [   ] or Unit Chief b6
[   ]   b7C

LEAD(s):

Set Lead 1:

   ALL RECEIVING OFFICES

(U) (S) Receiving offices are requested to provide FBIHQ with any threat-related information developed in your respective jurisdictions. In particular, Field Offices should task assets for any available information specifically relating to potential terrorist activity. Furthermore, those offices with border responsibilities and international airports are requested to review procedures with appropriate INS and USCS officials, as well as with other law enforcement agencies.

FEDERAL BUREAU OF INVESTIGATION
FOI/PA
DELETED PAGE INFORMATION SHEET
FOI/PA# 1165436-0

Total Deleted Page(s) = 20
Page 35 ~ Referral/Direct;
Page 36 ~ Referral/Direct;
Page 37 ~ Referral/Direct;
Page 38 ~ Referral/Direct;
Page 39 ~ Referral/Direct;
Page 40 ~ Referral/Direct;
Page 41 ~ Referral/Direct;
Page 42 ~ Referral/Direct;
Page 198 ~ Referral/Direct;
Page 199 ~ Referral/Direct;
Page 200 ~ Referral/Direct;
Page 201 ~ Referral/Direct;
Page 202 ~ Referral/Direct;
Page 208 ~ Referral/Consult;
Page 209 ~ Referral/Consult;
Page 210 ~ Referral/Consult;
Page 211 ~ Referral/Consult;
Page 216 ~ Referral/Consult;
Page 217 ~ Referral/Consult;
Page 218 ~ Referral/Consult;

```
XXXXXXXXXXXXXXXXXXXXXXXX
X    Deleted Page(s)      X
X    No Duplication Fee X
X    For this Page        X
XXXXXXXXXXXXXXXXXXXXXXXX
```

FEDERAL BUREAU OF INVESTIGATION

Precedence: ROUTINE   Date: 12/13/2000

To: Los Angeles   Attn: SA [   ]

    Counterterrorism   Attn: [   ]
                                   SSA [   ]
                                   SSA

From: New York
      [   ]
      Contact: SA [   ]

Approved By: [   ]

Drafted By: [   ]

(U)
Case ID #: (S) [   ]   (Pending)

Title: (U) (S) USAMA BIN LADEN
                IT-UBL/AL-QAEDA
                OO:NY
        (U)

Synopsis: (S) Request that additional New York personnel be granted ACS access to Los Angeles [   ] cases concerning UBL/Al-Qaeda.

(U) (S) Derived From : G-1
          Declassify On: X1

          (U)
Reference: (S) [   ]
           (S)
        (U)

Details: (S) In a communication dated 11/15/2000, Los Angeles (LA) granted New York personnel ACS access to the following [   ] case files:

[   ]

(U)
       (S) Since the date of the initial request made by New York, SA [   ] and IA [   ] have been designated to handle all intelligence related matters for Squad

SECRET

SEARCHED_____ INDEXED_____
SERIALIZED_____ FILED_____

DEC 1 5 2000

FBI — NEW YORK

To: Los Angeles   From: New York
Re: (☒) [§] [_____], 12/13/2000

[_____], SA [_____] and IA [_____] are the only individuals on New York's Terrorism Branch currently slated to review Islamic Army FISA matters which require certification and are subject to the "wall" which separates criminal vs. intelligence investigations. SA [_____] and IA [_____] will be the primary points of contact for intelligence matters for Squad [____].

(U)

To: Los Angeles   From: New York
Re: (S) [   ] , 12/13/2000

LEAD (s):

Set Lead 1:

LOS ANGELES

AT LOS ANGELES, CA

(U) [   ] (S) Request that ACS access be provided to SA [   ] and IA [   ] for all the UBL/Al-Qaeda related cases listed above.

◆◆

FEDERAL BUREAU OF INVESTIGATION

Precedence: ROUTINE   **Date:** 12/21/2000

To: Investigative Services   **Attn:** IOS, IOU II
                                              SSA ▢   b6
        Counterterrorism   **Attn:** ▢   SIOC/CAT A/B   b7C
                                                                            b7E

From: ▢
        Office of the Legal Attache
        Contact: ALAT ▢   b6
                                                                b7C
Approved By: ▢

Drafted By: ▢

(U) **Case ID #:** (S) ▢ ding)   b7E

(U) **Title:** (S) USAMA BIN LADEN/AL QAEDA   b3
                IT-UBL/AL-QAEDA
                OO:NY

Synopsis: (U) To respond to lead set forth in referenced
communication.

(U) (S)   **Classified By:** 7012, Legat/ ▢
               Reason   : 1.5(c)
               Declassify On: X1

(U) **Reference:** (S) ▢

(U) **Details:** (S) To date, Legat ▢ has developed no threat
related information. Should any information become available in
the future, Legat ▢ will promptly notify the
Counterterrorism Division.

        (U) Legat ▢ considers lead ▢
▢ covered.

To: Investigative Services From: [   ]

(U) Re: (S) [   ] 12/21/2000

LEAD(s):

Set Lead 1:

<u>ALL RECEIVING OFFICES</u>

(U) For information. Read and clear.

◆◆

FEDERAL BUREAU OF INVESTIGATION

Precedence: ROUTINE   Date: 09/27/2000

To: New York   Attn: SA [   ]

From: [   ]   b7E
      Squad [ ] JTTF
      Contact: SA [   ]

App[   ] [   ]y: [   ]   b6
                                                 b7C
Drafted By: [   ]

(U) Case ID #: (S) [   ] (Pending) b7E
                                           b3

(U) Title: (S) USAMA BIN LADIN;
               PAN HIZBALLAH;
               SAUDI HIZBALLAH;
               OTHER RADICAL ISLAMIC TERRORISM;
               [   ] DIVISION

Synopsis: (S) [   ]

(U) (S) Derived From: G-3
        Declassify On: X1

Details: (S) [   ]

[   ]

(U) (S) THIS INFORMATION IS PROVIDED BY A HIGHLY
SENSITIVE, SINGULAR SOURCE WHOSE ACCESS HAS PROVIDED RELIABLE AND
EXTREMELY PRODUCTIVE INFORMATION. INFORMATION FROM THIS ASSET
CANNOT BE DISSEMINATED OUTSIDE THE FBI WITHOUT CONSENT OF THE
[   ] DIVISION. ANY UNAUTHORIZED RELEASE OF THIS SENSITIVE
INFORMATION WILL JEOPARDIZE ESTABLISHED SOURCE AND METHODS.

SEARCHED ___ INDEXED ___
SERIALIZED ___ FILED ___

9

FBI — NEW YORK

(U) To: New York   From: [   ]
    Re: (S) [   ] 09/27/2000

♦♦0271[ ]01.ec

FEDERAL BUREAU OF INVESTIGATION

Precedence: ROUTINE   Date: 08/11/2000

To: New York   Attn: SA [   ]
                                  [   ] JTTF
                                  SLS [   ]
                                  [   ]

From: Washington Field
      [   ]
        Contact: SLS [   ]

Approved By: [   ]

Drafted By: [   ]

(U) Case ID #: (S) [   ]   b7A
               (U) [   ]   b3
                                                b7E

(S) Title: (S) TALIBAN;
               IT-OTHER (AFGHANISTAN)   b7E
               OO:NY

Synopsis: (S) [   ]

(U) (S)   Derived From : G-3   b1
               Declassify On: X1   b3
                                                b7E

[   ]

(U) Details: (S) THE INFORMATION SET FORTH IN THIS COMMUNICATION
WAS FURNISHED BY A HIGHLY SENSITIVE SOURCE OF KNOWN RELIABILITY.
INASMUCH AS THE INFORMATION PROVIDED IS SINGULAR IN NATURE,
EXTREME CAUTION SHOULD BE USED TO AVOID COMPROMISING THE IDENTITY
OF THE SOURCE.

(S) [   ]

[   ]

Our copy sent
from

b7E

AUG 15 2000

To: New York From: New York

Re: _____ 07/07/2000

b7A
b7E
b3

(S)

(S) This would definitely apply to USAMA BIN LADEN,

(S)

(S)

U.S. Department of Justice

Federal Bureau of Investigation

Legal Attache Office
Embassy of the United States
[   ] Saudi Arabia

20 December 2000

General Abdul Aziz Al-Huwairini
Ministry of Interior
Saudi Mabahith
Riyadh, Saudi Arabia

Subject: Interview of Usama Bin Laden (UBL)

Dear General Abdul Aziz:

As the holiest days of the Blessed month of Ramadan are celebrated, we continue to wish you and our Mabahith colleagues happy fasting and blessings and mercy from Allah.

Recently the Mabahith graciously provided [   ] with a videotape of an interview of UBL, which was sent to our offices in the U.S. Legat [   ] has since requested [   ] to obtain a copy of a taped interview of UBL on behalf of the Argentine Embassy in Washington, D.C. We believe both interviews are one and the same. In any event, we kindly ask your assistance in the following matter:

On 21 September 2000 the Al Jazeera channel broadcasted an interview of Usama Bin Laden conducted by Ahmad Muwaffaq Zaydan. It is alleged that during the interview, Bin Laden, Ayman Al Zawahiri and Rifai Taha promised to liberate the religious leader Sheikh Rahman, who is presently incarcerated in the U.S.

We kindly ask for the Mabahith's assistance in providing us with a copy of this interview, if possible, and extend our sincere thanks.

Sincerely

Legat Attache

① FOREIGN POLICE RELATIONS

①

DATE: *1/29/01*

TO: *New York*

FROM: LEGAT [ ]

RE: File number [ ]

Attached are the following original serials for your file.

_____

_____

_____

_____

_____

Copy to 265 NY...

... the ...
requested tape

b6
b7A
b7C

CC:

SUBJECT: REQUEST FOR VIDEO TAPE BROADCAST
PRIORITY: R
ATTACHMENTS:

      Date: 12/18/2000 12:02 pm (Monday)
      From: [ ]
        To: LEGAT [ ]
  Subject: REQUEST FOR VIDEO TAPE BROADCAST

PLEASE SEE ATTACHED REQUEST.

YOUR ASSISTANCE IN THIS MATTER WOULD BE GREATLY APPRECIATED.

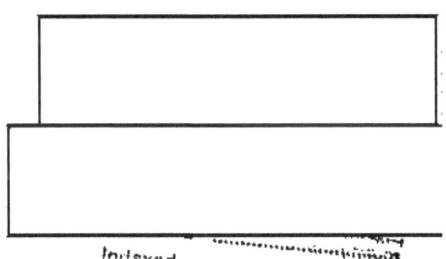

Indexed _____

12/18/00

Dear [ ]

    I am contacting you on the advice of Legat [ ] Legat [ ] advised that the below stated broadcast came out of your territory. This request is on behalf of the Argentine Embassy in Washington, D.C. who are seeking to obtain a video tape copy of an interview broadcasted by the "AL JAZEERA" channel on September 21, 2000, in Islamabad.

    On this date, AHMAD MUWAFFAQ ZAYDAN made a televised interview to OSMA BIN LADEN. BIN LADEN, together with AYMAN AL ZAWAHIRI and RIFAI TAHA would have promised to liberate the religious leader GAMA' AT AL ISLAMIYA, SHEIK RAHMAN, who is currently arrested in the United States. This promise was made through a video tape broadcasted by the "AL JAZERRA" channel.

    Thanking you in advance for your assistance in this matter.

[ ]
Liaison Analyst
International Operations Unit II
[ ]

FEDERAL BUREAU OF INVESTIGATION
FOI/PA
DELETED PAGE INFORMATION SHEET
FOI/PA# 1165436-0

Total Deleted Page(s) = 4
Page 227 ~ Referral/Consult;
Page 228 ~ Referral/Consult;
Page 229 ~ Referral/Consult;
Page 230 ~ Referral/Consult;

```
XXXXXXXXXXXXXXXXXXXXXXXX
X    Deleted Page(s)     X
X    No Duplication Fee  X
X    For this Page       X
XXXXXXXXXXXXXXXXXXXXXXXX
```

FEDERAL BUREAU OF INVESTIGATION

Precedence: PRIORITY   Date: 02/06/2001

To: Counterterrorism   Attn: Counterterrorism,
                                      SSA
                                      IOS
                                      IOS

    New York ✓②   Attn: Squad [   ] SSA [   ]
                                      SA
                                      SA

From: Los Angeles
            Contact: SA

Approved By:

Drafted By:

(U) Case ID #: ~~(S)~~
                ~~(S)~~

(U) Title: ~~(S)~~   TALIBAN;
                      IT-OTHER (AFGHANISTAN)

    (U) ~~(S)~~   USAMA BIN LADIN;
                   RELATED INTELLIGENCE INFORMATION;
                   IT-USAMA BIN LADIN (AL QAEDA)

Synopsis: (S)

        (U) ~~(S)~~   Derived From : G-3
                          Declassify On: X1

Administrative: (S)

(U) Details: ~~(S)~~   Reference e-mails and telephone calls between Los
Angeles, New York and Counterterrorism during weeks 1/22/2001 and

b3
b6
b7A

To: New York   From: ☒☒☒
Re: ☒ ☒☒☒☒☒☒☒ 04/20/2001

☒ Legat ☐ requests that FBINY in conjunction with ☐ provide an appropriate response ☐ to Legat ☐ for dissemination to ☐

To: New York From: [ ]

(U) Re: (X) [   ] 04/20/2001

LEAD(s):

Set Lead 1:

NEW YORK

AT NEW YORK, NY

(U) Provide an appropriate response to Legat [ ] for dissemination as outlined above.

Set Lead 2:

COUNTERTERRORISM

AT [   ] DC

(U) Coordinate response with [   ]

Set Lead 3: (adm)

ALL RECEIVING OFFICES

(U) Read and clear.

♦♦

SECRET

FEDERAL BUREAU OF INVESTIGATION

Precedence: ROUTINE   Date: 03/13/2001

To: Counterterrorism   Attn: UC ☐
                                          UC ☐

     Investigative Services   Attn: IOAU, IOU 2
     New York   Attn: SSA ☐
                                          Squad ☐

From: ☐
      Contact: ☐

Approved By: ☐

Drafted By: ☐

(U) Case ID #: (S) ☐ (Pending)

(U) Title: (S) USAMA BIN LADEN/AL-QAEDA
                IT-UBL/AL-QAEDA
                OO: NY

(U) Synopsis: (S) To provide a response to Lead ☐
Lead ☐ covered.

      (U) (S)   Classified By: 11532, ☐
                 Reason   : 1.5(c)
                 Declassify On: X-1   b3
                                                             b7E

(U) Reference: (S) ☐ Serial ☐

(U) Details: (S) In referenced communication, FBIHQ provided
background regarding threat information and requested the
recipients to provide FBIHQ with any threat-related information
developed in their respective jurisdictions.

      (U) (S) To date, ☐ has not developed any positive
information in this matter. However, FBIHQ should be secure in
the knowledge that ☐ has a continuing interest in this
matter and will expeditiously provide FBIHQ and New York with any
positive information received.

      (U) (S) In view of the foregoing, Lead ☐ is
considered covered.

SEARCHED _____   _____
SERIALIZED _____ FILED _____

MAY 2 2 2001

SECRET   b6
                                                             b7C

To: Counterterrorism From: [   ]

(U) Re: (X) [   ] 03/13/2001

b3
b7E

LEAD (s):

Set Lead 1:

ALL RECEIVING OFFICES

(U)   Please read and clear from ACS.

◆◆

SE~~CRET~~/~~ORCON~~/~~NOFORN~~

FEDERAL BUREAU OF INVESTIGATION

Precedence: IMMEDIATE   Date: 04/23/2001

To: Counterterrorism   Attn: [ ]   SSA [ ]
     New York   Attn: [ ]

From: Sacramento
        Squad [ ]
        Contact: SA [ ]

Approved By: [ ]

Drafted By: [ ]   13 [ ] 01.ec

(U) Case ID #: (S) [ ]   (Pending)

(U) Title: (S)   USAMA BIN LADEN;
                   IT-UBL/AL QAEDA

(U) Synopsis: (S)   To respond to lead set by the Bureau

        (U) (S)   Derived From : G-3
                        Declassify On: X1

(U) Reference: (S) [ ]   Serial [ ]   (04/13/2001)

(U) Details: (S/NF)   Referenced EC, dated 04/13/2001, advised
Sacramento of a heightened threat of terrorist attacks against
United States interests by Sunni extremists associated with Usama
Bin Laden. The communication also requested Sacramento to
provide any available reporting regarding current operational
activities relating to Sunni extremism.

        (U) (S)   Sacramento currently has no reporting for the
Bureau regarding this matter. If Sacramento should receive any
reporting, the information will be expeditiously provided to the
Bureau.

LEAD/ACTION/COVERED
DATE
ACTION
SUPV

APR 2 5 2001

SE~~CRET~~/~~ORCON~~/~~NOFORN~~

To: Counterterrorism From: Sacramento
(U) Re: (⊠) ⬚⬚⬚⬚⬚⬚⬚ 04/23/2001

LEAD(s):

Set Lead 1:

COUNTERTERRORISM

    AT WASHINGTON, DC

      (U) (⊠) ⬚⬚⬚⬚⬚⬚ , SSA ⬚⬚⬚⬚ is requested to read and clear.

Set Lead 2:

NEW YORK

    AT NEW YORK CITY

      (U) (⊠) Read and clear.

♦♦

FEDERAL BUREAU OF INVESTIGATION
FOI/PA
DELETED PAGE INFORMATION SHEET
FOI/PA# 1165436-0

Total Deleted Page(s) = 17
Page 27 ~ Referral/Direct;
Page 28 ~ Referral/Direct;
Page 29 ~ Referral/Direct;
Page 30 ~ Referral/Direct;
Page 31 ~ Referral/Direct;
Page 32 ~ Referral/Direct;
Page 33 ~ Referral/Direct;
Page 34 ~ Referral/Direct;
Page 354 ~ Referral/Consult;
Page 355 ~ Referral/Consult;
Page 356 ~ Referral/Consult;
Page 357 ~ Referral/Consult;
Page 358 ~ Referral/Consult;
Page 359 ~ Referral/Consult;
Page 360 ~ Referral/Consult;
Page 361 ~ Referral/Consult;
Page 362 ~ Referral/Consult;

```
XXXXXXXXXXXXXXXXXXXXXXXX
X    Deleted Page(s)    X
X    No Duplication Fee X
X    For this Page      X
XXXXXXXXXXXXXXXXXXXXXXXX
```

FEDERAL BUREAU OF INVESTIGATION

Precedence: ROUTINE   Date: 05/31/2001

To: Counterterrorism   Attn: ITOS/ [   ] SIOC CAT A & B
                                      SSA
                                      SSA
                                      IOS

     Phoenix   Attn: SSA
                                      SSA
                                      SA

From: New York
       Squad [   ]
       Contact: SA [   ]

Approved By: [   ]

Drafted By: [   ]

(U) Case ID #: (S) [   ] ~~(Pending)~~

(U) Title: (S) USAMA BIN LADEN;
                 IT-UBL/AL-QAEDA
                 OO:NY

(U) Synopsis: (S) To provide information from debrief of Phoenix
source in New York.

(U) (S)   Derived From : G-3
          Declassify On: X1

(U) Details: (S) Phoenix (PX) source was debriefed in New York with
representation of FBIHQ, Phoenix office and New York office.

(S) [   ]

SEARCHED_____ INDEXED_____
SERIALIZED_____ FILED_____

MAY 3 1 2001

FBI — NEW YORK

```
FEDERAL BUREAU OF INVESTIGATION
FOI/PA
DELETED PAGE INFORMATION SHEET
FOI/PA# 1165436-0

Total Deleted Page(s) = 28
Page 19 ~ Referral/Direct;
Page 20 ~ Referral/Consult;
Page 21 ~ Referral/Consult;
Page 22 ~ Referral/Consult;
Page 25 ~ Referral/Direct;
Page 26 ~ Referral/Direct;
Page 27 ~ Referral/Direct;
Page 33 ~ Referral/Direct;
Page 34 ~ Referral/Direct;
Page 35 ~ Referral/Direct;
Page 36 ~ Referral/Direct;
Page 37 ~ Referral/Consult;
Page 38 ~ Referral/Consult;
Page 39 ~ Referral/Consult;
Page 40 ~ Referral/Consult;
Page 41 ~ Referral/Consult;
Page 47 ~ Referral/Direct;
Page 48 ~ Referral/Direct;
Page 49 ~ Referral/Direct;
Page 57 ~ Referral/Direct;
Page 58 ~ Referral/Direct;
Page 59 ~ Referral/Direct;
Page 60 ~ Referral/Direct;
Page 61 ~ Referral/Direct;
Page 62 ~ Referral/Direct;
Page 63 ~ Referral/Direct;
Page 64 ~ Referral/Direct;
Page 65 ~ Referral/Direct;
```

```
XXXXXXXXXXXXXXXXXXXXXXXX
X    Deleted Page(s)     X
X    No Duplication Fee  X
X    For this Page       X
XXXXXXXXXXXXXXXXXXXXXXXX
```

FD-36 (Rev. 8-29-85)

FBI

TRANSMIT VIA:	PRECEDENCE:	CLASSIFICATION:
☒ Teletype	☐ Immediate	☐ TOP SECRET
☐ Facsimile	☒ Priority	☒ ~~SECRET~~
☐ AIRTEL	☐ Routine	☐ CONFIDENTIAL
		☐ UNCLAS E F T O
		☐ UNCLAS

Date 1/2/97

FM LEGAT [ ] (P)

TO DIRECTOR FBI/PRIORITY/

FBI NEW YORK [ ] /PRIORITY/

BT

~~SECRET~~

CITE: //5250[ ]96.002//

PASS: FBIHQ, ATTN: NSD, SSA [ ] SA [ ]

[ ]

(U) SUBJECT: (S) OSAMA BIN LADIN, AKA USAMA BIN LADEN; IT -

SUDAN; OO: NY.

(U) (S) REQUEST OF THE BUREAU:

(S)

| Approved | | Original filename: | 596W.002 |
| Time Rec | | Telprep filename: | 59650.002 |

MRI/JULIAN DATE: _____ ISN: _____

(S)

D - 1736   5 mars 1998

SUBJECT: OSAMA BIN LADIN

Our Headquarters has provided us with the following
information for you:

Usama Bin Ladin is one of the most significant sponsors of
Islamic extremists activities in the world today. He is the son
of Saudi construction magnate Muhammad Bin Ladin, founder of the
Saudi Arabian Bin Ladin Group business empire.

Bin Ladin joined the Afghan resistance movement almost
immediately following the 12/26/79 Soviet invasion of
Afghanistan. He gained prominence during the Afghan war for his
role in financing the recruitment, transportation and training of
Arab nationals who volunteered to fight alongside the Afghan
mujahedin.

Following the withdrawal of the Soviets from Afghanistan in
1989, Bin Ladin continued to support militant Islamic groups who
had begun to target moderate Islamic governments in the region.
Bin Ladin drew on his family's wealth to organize these extremist
groups and fund camps in Afghanistan and Pakistan to provide new
recruits with paramilitary training.

Saudi officials seized Bin Ladin's passport from 1989 until
1991 in an attempt to prevent him from combining forces with
extremists whom he met during the Afghan war. He relocated to
Sudan in 1991.

In February 1994, Saudi Arabia revoked Bin Ladin's Saudi
citizenship for behavior that "contradicts the Kingdom's
interests and risks harming its relations with fraternal
countries"

As Bin Ladin's business interests expanded so did his
financial support for Islamic extremist groups.

Bin Ladin formed a London-based dissident organization in
July 1995, called the "Advisory and Reformation Committee," which
has issued pamphlets critical of the Saudi Government.

Pakistani investigators noted in March 1995 that Ramzi Ahmad
Yousef, the terrorist who masterminded the 1993 World Trade
Center bombing, resided at a Bin Ladin funded guesthouse in
Peshawar during most of the three years before his apprehension.

A leading member of the Egyptian extremist group al-Jihad, claimed in a July 1995 interview with Egyptian journalists that Bin Ladin helped fund al-Jihad and was at times aware of specific terrorist operations mounted by the group against Egyptian interests. According to alleged terrorists, recently captured by Egyptian authorities, Bin Ladin also remains the key financier behind the "Kunar" camp in Afghanistan which provides terrorist training to al-Jihad and Al-Gamma al-Islamiyyah members.

In early 1996 Bin Ladin was asked to leave Sudan at which time he moved to Afghanistan where he remains today.

In a May 1997 interview with Bin Ladin, he declared jihad against the U.S. Government. He stated that his group had focused his declaration of jihad against soldiers in the country of the two holy places (Saudi Arabia). He went on to say that even though American civilians are not targeted they must leave.

Bin Ladin's support for extremist causes has continued despite criticisms from regional governments. Algeria, Egypt and Yemen have accused Bin Ladin of financing militant Islamic groups in their own countries.

Bin Ladin has publicly claimed credit for the bombing of the OPM Sang facility in Saudi Arabia and the attack on U.S. servicemen in Somalia during Operation Restore Hope. Bin Ladin recently joined with several other terrorist organizations in issuing a FATWA urging Muslims to strike and kill U.S. citizens everywhere as a religious duty.

v - 4272   5 mars 1998

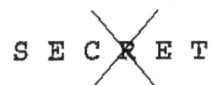

FEDERAL BUREAU OF INVESTIGATION
FOI/PA
DELETED PAGE INFORMATION SHEET
FOI/PA# 1165436-0

Total Deleted Page(s) = 9
Page 16 ~ b1; b3;
Page 17 ~ b1; b3;
Page 18 ~ b1; b3;
Page 19 ~ b1; b3;
Page 20 ~ b1; b3;
Page 21 ~ b1; b3;
Page 22 ~ b1; b3;
Page 23 ~ b1; b3;
Page 24 ~ b1; b3;

XXXXXXXXXXXXXXXXXXXXXXXX
X   Deleted Page(s)   X
X   No Duplication Fee X
X   For this Page   X
XXXXXXXXXXXXXXXXXXXXXXXX

FD-340b (Rev. 8-7-97)

Universal Case File Number

Field Office Acquiring Evidence _____

Serial # of Originating Document _4427_

Date Received _11-5-01_

From _Legat_ _____
                    (Name of Contributor)

_____
           (Address of Contributor)

By _ALAT_ _____
                    (Name of Special Agent)

To Be Returned   ☐ Yes ☐ No

Receipt Given   ☐ Yes ☑ No

Grand Jury Material - Disseminate Only Pursuant

to Rule 6 (e), Federal Rules of Criminal Procedure

☐ Yes ☐ No

Title: UBL

Reference: _____
                    (Communication Enclosing Material)

_____

Description: ☐ Original notes re interview of

(S)

FEDERAL BUREAU OF INVESTIGATION
FOI/PA
DELETED PAGE INFORMATION SHEET
FOI/PA# 1165436-0

Total Deleted Page(s) = 14
Page 19 ~ Referral/Consult;
Page 20 ~ Referral/Consult;
Page 21 ~ Referral/Consult;
Page 22 ~ Referral/Consult;
Page 23 ~ Referral/Consult;
Page 24 ~ Referral/Consult;
Page 25 ~ Referral/Consult;
Page 26 ~ Referral/Consult;
Page 27 ~ Referral/Consult;
Page 28 ~ Referral/Consult;
Page 29 ~ Referral/Consult;
Page 30 ~ Referral/Consult;
Page 31 ~ Referral/Consult;
Page 32 ~ Referral/Consult;

```
XXXXXXXXXXXXXXXXXXXXXXXX
X    Deleted Page(s)      X
X    No Duplication Fee X
X    For this Page        X
XXXXXXXXXXXXXXXXXXXXXXXX
```

FEDERAL BUREAU OF INVESTIGATION
FOI/PA
DELETED PAGE INFORMATION SHEET
FOI/PA# 1165436-0

Total Deleted Page(s) = 19
Page 252 ~ Referral/Consult;
Page 253 ~ Referral/Consult;
Page 254 ~ Referral/Consult;
Page 255 ~ Referral/Consult;
Page 256 ~ Referral/Consult;
Page 257 ~ Referral/Consult;
Page 258 ~ Referral/Consult;
Page 259 ~ Referral/Consult;
Page 260 ~ Referral/Consult;
Page 270 ~ Referral/Consult;
Page 271 ~ Referral/Consult;
Page 272 ~ Referral/Consult;
Page 273 ~ Referral/Consult;
Page 274 ~ Referral/Consult;
Page 275 ~ Referral/Consult;
Page 276 ~ Referral/Consult;
Page 277 ~ Referral/Consult;
Page 278 ~ Referral/Consult;
Page 279 ~ Referral/Consult;

```
XXXXXXXXXXXXXXXXXXXXXXXX
X    Deleted Page(s)     X
X    No Duplication Fee  X
X    For this Page       X
XXXXXXXXXXXXXXXXXXXXXXXX
```

SECRET

FEDERAL BUREAU OF INVESTIGATION

Precedence: ROUTINE   Date: 02/22/1999

To: New York

From: New York Div I

       Contact:

Approved By:

Drafted By:

(U) Case ID #: (S)   (Pending)
                (S)   (Pending)

(U) Title: (S)   OSAMA BIN LADIN
                 IT-SUDAN
                 OO:NY   Subfile:
                               Miscellaneous Matters

(U) Synopsis: (S)   Open a Miscellaneous sub file in captioned matter
to maintain information on assorted   matters, to include
                         by other field offices regarding
captioned subject.

(U) (S)   Derived From : G-1
           Declassify On: X-1

(U) Details: (S)   It is requested that a Miscellaneous sub file
) be opened regarding captioned matter.
This file will maintain in an organized fashion information on
assorted   matters, to include
             by other field offices regarding captioned subject.

       (U) (S)   New subfile :

1.
(1)
(2)
                       UPLOADED

                           2-3-99

◆◆

misfile

SECRET

(U) To: New York From: Los Angeles
Re: (S) [   ] 12/14/2000

LEAD(s):

Set Lead 1:

NEW YORK

AT NEW YORK, NEW YORK

(U) Read and clear.

Set Lead 2:

COUNTERTERRORISM

AT WASHINGTON, DC

(U) Read and clear.

◆◆

Details: (S/OC/NF) There have been claims of responsibility by four
(U) groups regarding the October 12, 2000, attack on the USS Cole.
Those groups include the Islamic Army of Aden, Islamic Deterrent
Forces, Mohammad's Army and the Organization of the Oppressed in Jabal
Amil. Like previous suspected Usama Bin Laden-sponsored attacks in
East Africa in 1998, and planned attacks in Jordan in 1999, the United
States was the intended target for an attack designed to bring about
the deaths of American citizens. In totality, two hundred and
forty-one (241) persons, including 31 Americans, were killed in the
terrorist bombings in Kenya and Yemen.

(U) In addition to targeting U.S. interests overseas,
terrorists operating in support of the international jihad movement have
also conducted acts of terrorism on U.S. soil. Specifically, on February
26, 1993, Islamic extremists of various nationalities aligned with
Sheikh Omar Abdel Rahman, spiritual leader of the Egyptian Al Gama Al
Islamiyya (AGAI) and the Egyptian Islamic Jihad (EIJ), bombed the World
Trade Center (WTC) in New York City. Six persons were killed and another
1,000 were injured in this attack. Subsequent to this attack, the FBI
thwarted a plot in June 1993 by other Islamic extremists operating under
the guidance of Sheikh Rahman to bomb several targets in the New York
metropolitan area. Prior to this time, the United States appeared
invulnerable to international terrorist activity on U.S. soil.

(S/NF) In addition, the FBI investigation regarding Ahmed
Ressam and his attempt to enter the United States in December, 1999,
continues. As receiving offices are aware, on December 14, 1999, Ressam
was arrested after attempting to enter the United States at the Port
Angeles, Washington, point of entry. Ressam, who was carrying multiple
forms of identification in varying names, was transporting items which
could be used to make several explosive devices. To date, Ressam's
target(s) in the United States are unknown. It is also unknown how many
others were involved in the plot, and the organizational structure of
the group of individuals associated with this case. In addition, it is
unknown if Ressam was acting on behalf of a specific terrorist
group/sponsor. Ressam and some of his conspirators have been linked to
the overall Sunni Islamic extremists network.

(X/NF) Guided by radical spiritual leaders, such as Sheikh Rahman, and extremist Islamic benefactors, such as UBL, terrorist attacks conducted by the international jihad movement are increasingly overshadowing attacks conducted by other terrorist groups and state sponsors. Further, the level of sophistication and lethality of attacks has significantly increased over the years. This is believed to be attributed to the conjoin of former Arab-Afghan mujahadeen with extensive explosives and combat experience into a movement dedicated to international jihad. The well-planned attack on the USS Cole, a U.S. Navy destroyer, is indicative of the capabilities and impudence of this movement and its members/supporters.

(U) (X/NF) In response to the attack on the USS Cole and the continuing threat posed by UBL and other terrorists operating within the framework of the international jihad movement, a number of disruption operations have been initiated overseas. Intelligence gleaned, thus far, from these operations indicates that the United States continues to be a primary target for attack by UBL and his supporters. In addition, intelligence suggests that there may be plans for additional attacks targeting U.S. interests. To date, however, the FBI is not in receipt of any specific target, location or time frame for reported UBL-supported attack(s). Nevertheless, disruption operations in the past have resulted in terrorist reprisals. As an example, in October 1995, the AGAI claimed responsibility for the suicide car bombing of local police headquarters in Rijeka, Croatia. This attack was in response to the detainment of an AGAI leader in Croatia. Further, in mid-November 1999, the FBI received information indicating that a Yemen-based UBL-aligned terrorist and unidentified terrorists residing in Pakistan had made plans to bomb U.S. targets in Saudi Arabia and Yemen. No specific U.S. targets were mentioned. The attacks, which ultimately were not carried out, were reportedly planned to retaliate for the execution of a Sunni extremist leader in Yemen.

(S/NF) In addition to the potential threat posed by UBL and the international jihad movement, events currently unfolding in the world arena, such as the ongoing crisis in the Middle East, could portend potential acts of anti-U.S. terrorism by other Islamic extremists. Recently, the FBI learned that Egyptian AGAI leader [ ] [ ] who perceives the United States as pro-Israel, has called upon Islamic extremists worldwide to target American and Israeli interests. Specifically, on September 13, 2000, [ ] supra, issued a statement calling for Muslims to "liberate" Jerusalem, while at the same time, threatened U.S. interests in the Middle East. In the statement, [ ] clearly voiced his opposition to the "sharing of Jerusalem with Israel" and stated "we reject the possibility of giving up one inch of Muslim Palestine, to say nothing of Jerusalem." [ ] went on to say, "the United States must realize that the idolatrous paper-thin regime of the region will not be able to protect themselves from the anger of our people." "They must also realize that no one will be able to protect their interests in the region as long as they continue their double standards." [ ] concluded his statement with "raining down painful blows on Jews and Americans must constitute one of the most important religious duties for every able Muslim." In addition, intelligence indicates that the Jerusalem issue is paramount to UBL supporters because it signifies the Americans are crusaders.

(S/NF) Further exacerbating the potential terrorist threat in the near term is the advent of Ramadan, the Muslim holy month of fasting, which begins circa November 27, 2000 and ends in late December 2000. In the past, Islamic extremists have engaged in violent acts of terrorism during this time period, particularly on the "Night of Power." According to Muslim tradition, "Laylatul Qadr" or the Night of Power, aka the Night of Destiny, represents the date when Allah first revealed the Quran to Muhammad. Also, on this night the gates of heaven are said to be open, sins are forgiven and prayers are answered for all those who pray. (Note: Muslim tradition dictates that the "Night of Power" occurs during the last ten days of Ramadan. During 1999, Ramadan was observed December 9, 1999 through January 7, 2000 and the Night of Power is believed to have been observed on January 4, 2000.) The "Night of Power" this year could fall on/about December 25, 2000.

(U//NF) In order to adequately address the potential threat emanating from UBL/Al Qaeda and the international jihad movement, recipients are requested to provide FBIHQ with any threat-related information developed in your respective offices. In furtherance of this effort, field offices should task assets for any available information specifically relating to potential terrorist activity. In addition, those field offices with border responsibilities and international airports are requested to review procedures with appropriate officials of the INS, USCS, and other law enforcement entities.

(U//NF) To reiterate, FBIHQ is currently not in receipt of any specific information to indicate that a UBL/Al Qaeda terrorist attack is imminent. However, given the present state of global affairs and intelligence indicating the United States remains a primary target for UBL and other Islamic extremists, the potential for anti-U.S. terrorist activity exists. Further, upcoming special events that afford widespread media coverage, particularly the Presidential Inauguration and the Super Bowl, could be attractive targets for such activity. You will be advised of additional information as it becomes available.

(U)   Questions regarding this communication should be directed to Unit Chief ██████████████████████████ or Unit Chief ████████████████████████

ALL RECEIVING OFFICES

(U//X) Receiving offices are requested to provide FBIHQ with any threat-related information developed in your respective jurisdictions. In particular, Field Offices should task assets for any available information specifically relating to potential terrorist activity. Furthermore, those offices with border responsibilities and international airports are requested to review procedures with appropriate INS and USCS officials, as well as with other law enforcement agencies.

SECRET